MW01001883

BANK ON IT!

BANK ON IT!

A GUIDE TO MUTUAL BANK CONVERSIONS-
A HIDDEN GEM WITHIN TODAY'S
INVESTMENT LANDSCAPE

Tim M. Rooney CFP®

ISBN: 0692891455
ISBN-13: 9780692891452
Library of Congress Control Number: 2017907764
Bank On IT!, Fort Wayne IN

PREFACE

I have been a financial adviser for more than thirty years. I have seen many investment strategies used to provide above-average returns. I have had clients invest in speculative investments such as options and commodities. Others have used margin and leverage to enhance their returns. I have seen clients buy small cap, large cap, and value stocks in an attempt to achieve higher returns. Still others have invested in gold and silver, penny stocks, private placements, and hedge funds in an attempt to outperform other investors. I never thought a deposit I made in my local savings bank would lead to an investment strategy that would enable me to become a multimillionaire. This book will describe in detail my investment thesis, which I believe is one of the best opportunities available today. I will describe how my career began and has evolved over the past thirty years, and how I found the idea of investing in mutual bank conversions. I will explain how these conversions work and how to participate in them. I will also give advice on the many investments I have seen as a financial adviser for over three decades. I am writing this book in honor of my children, so they can also think outside the box in whatever endeavors they may choose.

TABLE OF CONTENTS

CHAPTER 1

My Early Years

I was raised in Fort Wayne, Indiana, the second largest city in the state with a population of around two hundred seventy thousand. Indiana is a fairly conservative, Midwestern state with many friendly people. It is a very flat state with a large number of farmlands, and is home to the Indianapolis 500 and the University of Notre Dame, along with Indiana and Purdue Universities. When I grew up in Indiana, families did not worry about locking doors and genuinely tried to help one another. The people of Indiana value hard work and believe a person's word is his/her bond. Name and reputation are prized possessions. In most presidential elections, Indiana is the first red state to appear on the electoral map in the Republican's win column, which shows the state's conservative values. Indiana is also known for its basketball roots: Larry Bird began his career here and Bobby Knight won three national championships at Indiana University. Fort Wayne had one of the original NBA teams in the 1950s before they moved to Detroit. The basketball movie *Hoosiers* depicts many of these Indiana values. John Mellencamp's song lyric "I was born in a small town" depicts most of the cities in Indiana. This small-town environment created a more laid-back atmosphere and a sense of closeness among communities and neighborhoods. Many jobs were based in the manufacturing sector and produced cars, trucks, and RVs. Northern Indiana has some large lakes and vast areas of farmland, and corn and soybean crops are found in most of the state's rural areas. Southern Indiana has more hills than the flat areas around Fort Wayne.

I was raised as the youngest of three siblings. My brother, Pat, was the oldest child and today oversees many shopping malls in Chicago. My sister, Ann, is four years older than me and teaches school in Fort Wayne. My father owned his own small business as a manufacturer's rep selling gas logs and fireplaces to Midwestern retailers. My mother raised us at home and hung wallpaper on the side to help pay for our Catholic education. We attended Saint Jude grade school, which had a convent of nuns who were teachers and administrators at the school. We also attended a Catholic high school. Both schools had a dress code where girls wore skirts and boys a shirt and tie. This discipline at an early age was a good foundation for creating a solid work ethic in adulthood.

I grew up playing many sports. We lived in a neighborhood where houses were right next to one another. We would play Wiffle Ball, football, and basketball with many neighborhood friends. There were no cell phones or video games. We would constantly be outside doing some physical activity with our friends. Today's kids are missing out on the interaction we had in the 1970s and1980s. We would much rather have played outside than stayed inside our homes. I believe this lack of physical activity in our youth is one of the reasons we have an obesity problem in America. During my youth I played a lot of basketball, which was by far the most popular sport in Indiana. I attended Bobby Knight's basketball camps in Bloomington during middle school summers. In high school I also ran track and cross-country, and my fastest mile time was 4:34. I still run today. Until I had a hip replacement a year ago, I was still able to win my age group in most of the 5 and 10K races I ran. I still try to work out almost every day of the week. This discipline for delayed gratification plays a role in my mutual-bank investment thesis. Sports can give a child many life-learning experiences that he or she can use later in life. Sports teach that you will not always win in life. An individual can work on their mistakes and learn to succeed next time.

My father was on the road for many weeks during my grade school and high school years. He traveled around a ten-state radius to sell his gas logs and fire-places. By the time I was in high school, my brother and sister were off at college. My brother graduated from Indiana State University the year Larry Bird played Magic Johnson in the NCAA finals. My sister attended Ball State University, the alma mater of David Letterman. During this time I spent many weeks alone with my mother. Many friends used to congregate at our house during high school. It was fondly referred to as the "Hotel" by many of my classmates. We created our own Wrigley Field to play Wiffle Ball between the neighbors' houses. In my high school years, I was an above-average student; however, my focus was more centered on hanging out with my friends and playing sports than pursuing straight A's in the classroom. I have many fond memories of the fun I had during my high school years. We had a softball team called the Sessions (named for our constant parties), and we would play against much older men in competitive leagues. It took us a year to win our first game! We had a keg of beer behind the dugout during some of the games, and the stands would be packed with girlfriends laughing at us. We had so much fun that I did not want to see those years end.

During my senior year in 1980, I decided to attend Purdue University. Looking back I do not know why I chose to attend Purdue—probably because in high school I was having so much fun that proper

University evaluation did not take place. I did not research various colleges as today's students do. Purdue was a state school about two hours from Fort Wayne, and in the 1980's it was pretty easy to get accepted to the state universities. Today you have to have very high grades and high SAT/ACT scores to get in these schools. To this day many people have told me they thought of Purdue as an Ivy League-type education.

During my freshman year at Purdue, I resided in a dormitory called Cary Quad. This was the oldest residence hall on campus. My room was the size of a prison cell and I had to share it with a roommate. During this time I realized what it must have felt like to be a prisoner at Alcatraz! The demographics of Purdue students in 1980 were four men to every one woman. After having such a fun social life in high school, I found my surroundings at Purdue not as enjoyable. Purdue was a very fraternity-focused campus. I remember going to a rush party and was not a fan of the hazing that took place. Having gone to parties all through high school, I could not understand having eggs thrown at me being a requirement to attend a party! Today many friends have told me that I would have had a much more enjoyable social life if I had joined a fraternity while at Purdue. After my prison sentence in Cary Quad during my freshman year, I lived in apartments my final three years, and I found myself studying more. In hindsight this lack of social life was probably the best thing that could have happened to me.

With a limited social life at Purdue, I began to concentrate more on my classes. I soon made the dean's list and carried a 5.8 GPA on a 6.0 scale. After each year I thought about transferring to a school with more girls and a better social life. But if I transferred, my credits would transfer but not my grades. I knew if I continued to maintain a high GPA, I could get a good-paying job upon graduation. Thus, I remained at Purdue for four years. Like many college students, I did not know what I wanted to pursue as a career path. During my senior year, I took an investments course that changed my career outlook. This was a course that truly clicked with me. Many of the topics we discussed could translate into my everyday life. I learned many different types of investment vehicles individuals have to choose from, and the risk/reward of each different opportunity. The course I took at Purdue opened my eyes to how the investment world works. Many courses students take today do not provide them with the essential tools and information they need to use in everyday life. In high school, my children were not taught basic concepts such as how to balance a checkbook or how the cost of interest will affect them in buying a house. Instead they learn geometry and algebra, which seldom are used in anyone's daily routine.

During the summer months while at college, I worked on the line at our local bread and bun manufacturer back home in Fort Wayne. This was a very demanding physical job. I still today have burn marks from taking off the hot pans when the production line stopped. We had to pull the racks out of a pressurized area and drag them to another worker who would manually load the pans into the oven. Today this factory is totally automated. Thus, many of these summertime positions no longer exist. These advancements in technology and automation are one of the reasons we have fewer manufacturing jobs in America. This hard summer job made me realize that I needed to attain a college degree to get a high-paying job with a significant future. This past summer my oldest son worked at a local bakery to realize the same thing.

I graduated from Purdue with high honors. One of Purdue's strengths was that it had a fantastic placement department. (I encourage all parents to check out this feature when they are searching for the right college for their children to attend. It makes no sense to attend college and leave without a job opportunity. Have your kids look for internships while in college. These internships could lead to a job offer after graduation. Just graduating with a degree and no experience is not enough in today's competitive work environment.) I contemplated going to law school and visited my older cousin in Chicago to discuss this endeavor. He had me talk to several of his classmates and other attorneys. I was told that less than 50 percent of his graduating class in law school actually became attorneys. I could not see going to school for another three years and not being assured that I would attain a job. I had five job offers from participating in Purdue's placement interviews. I investigated jobs in the investment industry, but I was told that I needed a few years' experience in sales before I could get into the industry. From the five offers I received, I took the job offer that paid me the highest salary. I became a cost analyst at General Foods in Lafayette, Indiana.

At General Foods, I was given the Stove Top Stuffing line to follow through production. I tracked cost variances and created monthly production reports. I enjoyed presenting my reports on Stove Top at monthly meetings. Most of my time was spent at a desk crunching numbers on a calculator. I continued to work at General Foods for almost two years. During one of my reviews, my supervisor said that I could stay there forever, but she did not think the job suited my personality. I enjoyed interacting with people much more than the accounting aspect of this job. Verifying and crunching numbers was not overly exciting for me, so this advice was very helpful to me pursuing a new career path.

A headhunter recruited me for a similar position in my hometown of Fort Wayne at North American Van Lines. During the moving process I moved my stock account I had accumulated from working over the summer months during college back to a broker in Fort Wayne at Shearson Lehman Brothers. I had previously asked him about becoming an adviser upon graduating from Purdue. Upon my return home, he asked me if I was still interested in entering the brokerage business. He said that they had a trainee position open at the firm. At my new job at North American Van Lines, I felt limited upside and advancement potential similar to what I had experienced at General Foods. I decided to take the offer to become a trainee at Shearson in 1986. I struggled initially with the decision to give up a salary to try a commission-based job. But an old friend who is now deceased told me, "Roon, the forty-thousand dollar-a-year jobs will be there for you if this does not work out." I took his advice and took the trainee position.

During the Shearson interviewing process, I flew to Chicago with a fellow trainee. He had an introverted personality. I knew right away that I could interact with people better than he could. I was only twenty-four years old when I started as a Shearson trainee. During the first three months, my only requirement was to study and pass the Series 7 test. Trainees were fired if they failed to pass the exam. I practically stayed at home for three months and did nothing but study to ensure I would pass this test. I passed the exam with an eighty-eight out of one hundred. I then spent six weeks in Chicago with twenty-four other trainees from around the country. We had classes from eight to five o'clock five days a week. Part of this training was investment product training. However, most of the training was on how to sell. I was the youngest trainee in the class. Most of the other trainees were in their mid-forties trying to pursue a second career. One was a former Penn State football player, but most were older men trying a new occupation. I had just graduated from college, but that six weeks reminded me of the movie *Animal House*. After classes, there were trips to many bars for upside-down margarita shots. There were wrestling matches in the apartment rooms. Our class of twenty-four was a class they called Miss Hires! After the six weeks, the trainee director had called our local manager to say that everyone should be fired! Today only two of us from that trainee class are still in the investment industry, and we surprisingly both work at the same firm today, Stifel.

I vividly remember us cold-calling as a way to open new accounts. We would call a list of investors typically with a municipal bond that paid an attractive yield and try to open as many accounts as possible. In the '80s and '90s, cold-calling was the main way to develop a clientele. Today, with many do-not-call lists, it is much more difficult to use this strategy to access clients. Today any young, aspiring individual looking to become a financial adviser typically joins an existing team.

Anyone who has started from scratch in the brokerage industry knows it is an uphill battle to develop a clientele. I was fortunate to know many people in my hometown. Another advantage of starting out at a larger brokerage firm is that many advisers fail. When this happens their accounts are dispersed among the remaining brokers. When other advisers would leave the firm, I did very well in retaining these relationships.

The keys to being a successful broker are honesty, determination, and a strong work ethic. It typically takes an adviser three to five years to develop a large enough client base to know that he or she will succeed. Through many cold calls, seminars, and hard work, I developed a successful book of clients. Most of these clients were small business owners, successful executives, and retirees. Any clientele business is based on referrals. If an individual likes who cuts his or her hair, they will refer their friends. It is the same with the brokerage industry: if you do well for your clients, they will send you referrals. An adviser will get referrals if he or she stays committed to the plan he or she has developed for his or her clients. Semiannual or annual reviews are a must. Many advisers in the financial industry will sell an investor some investment products and not call him or her again. Clients want investment ideas. They also want their adviser to stay in contact with them. An adviser needs to differentiate him- or herself from the competition. Any investor can go online and buy a mutual fund or a stock. The successful adviser needs to develop a meaningful diversified plan for his or her clients. This will lead to an abundance of referrals.

It took me about six to seven years to realize I was going to be able to make a career as a financial adviser. I was finally developing a significant asset base of clients. I had become comfortable in understanding the many nuances of the investment products available. I was very comfortable interacting with clients. After seven years at Shearson, which became Smith Barney in a merger, I was qualifying for the company's president's and then chairman's council. These were production recognition levels for the most successful advisers at the firm. I finally was on my way to developing a successful career.

CHAPTER 2

OPENING AND PARTICIPATING IN MY FIRST
BANK IPO

I t is a constant learning experience in any financial adviser's beginning years to grasp all of the intricacies of the financial markets. It takes time to anticipate changes in the marketplace. There are many investment products to understand and be able to explain to clients. Investors typically think of stocks and bonds when thinking of investment vehicles. But advisers must understand options, margin requirements, syndicate, and many other investment vehicles to offer their clientele. A successful adviser needs to differentiate himself from others. Any investor can buy a mutual fund or stock on his or her own. An adviser must bring value and added insight to his or her clients. I always was more in tune with following the markets and recommending individual stocks than most of my peers. Many advisers pick money managers and mutual funds to manage their growth investments. I enjoyed picking and finding stock ideas for my clients. I truly liked to develop a portfolio that met the investor's needs and goals. Every investor has different risk tolerances. It is up to the adviser to understand that and provide solutions that will meet the investor's risk levels.

In 1992, six years into the business, a friend told me that he heard that our local bank, Home Loan Savings, might be going public in the near future. He had heard that most local bank savings were attractive investments. I began to research the idea. I found an article in the October 1992 edition of *Worth* magazine by Peter Lynch stating that one's local bank may be one of the best investment opportunities an individual can make. Peter Lynch made his name as the manager of one of Fidelity's largest mutual funds. He grew the Fidelity Magellan Fund into one of the largest funds in the industry by looking for undervalued companies to buy.

Peter Lynch noted that one could participate in a local bank's IPO just by becoming a depositor at the bank. He went on to explain how the returns on these stock offerings have been dramatically better than market returns to date.

I went to the library and found a savings and loan publication, now called *SNL Digest*, that had the history of past local savings bank conversions. The results of the stock performance on these conversions were amazing. Most had gone up 20 to 40 percent from their offering price within their first few weeks of trading. The longer-term results were even better. After seeing this, I opened a CD at Home Loan Savings Bank in Fort Wayne. I did not know when the bank would issue stock, but I wanted an opportunity to participate in the IPO if they did decide to issue stock to their depositors.

An IPO, or initial public offering, is an opportunity for an investor to become a charter shareholder of a company as it enters the public marketplace. There are primary and secondary offerings. A primary offering is an initial offering to begin trading on a public exchange (such as the NYSE or NASDAQ exchange), and a secondary offering is when a company issues additional shares to the already public marketplace. The bank offerings I wanted to participate in were the primary or initial stock offerings. Henceforth, I will use the term *IPO* to describe these types of offerings.

The problem with most IPOs is that it is very hard for an individual or retail investor to participate in these investments. If the company is classified as a hot IPO (which means there is a good chance that the share price will rise when it begins publicly trading), it is hard for most investors to get even one hundred shares of the offering. The whole allocation process of IPOs has bothered me through-out my career. Underwriters typically give share allo-cations mainly to institutional accounts and regional funds. Institutional accounts and mutual funds usu-ally have larger accounts at these investment firms that underwrite new IPOs. They also participate in about every deal the firm brings to the marketplace. Thus, institutional accounts take the bad and the good deals. So, this is the reason the small investor will get very few shares allocated to them.

Years ago, Google created their IPO by holding a Dutch auction that gave individuals a better shot at getting shares of their IPO. These investors put bids in at the various prices they were willing to pay to acquire shares of Google in the stock offer. I wish more companies would do this or create a way for the small investor to get larger share allocations in future IPOs. And if for some reason you do receive a large allocation from your firm's syndicate depart-ment, those IPO offerings typically do not work out in the small investors' favor. The past Facebook offering is a prime example. Our brokerage firm received an above-average allocation in the stock of-fering. The stock opened at $38 and then proceed-ed to decline to $19 six months later. Now Facebook trades at $118. So patient, long-term holders of this IPO have been greatly rewarded, but initial investors looking for the quick gain were disappointed. Long-term patience is the key to establishing substantial long-term returns. This long-term patience is need-ed to get the maximum return on these bank mu-tual conversions. Many of these banks that convert and go public are often bought by a larger institu-tion after three to five years. It is very hard to trade in and out of a long-term stock holding. An investor needs to make two correct decisions when trading stocks. The first is to sell at a price he or she thinks is at a peak, and the second is being able to buy the same stock back at a lower price than he or she sold it at. This is very difficult to do on a stock that has been a great long-term investment.

It would have been a bad decision to sell Amazon, Google, Visa, or most quality names instead of hold-ing the shares for the long-term wealth creation. Case in point is this year's 2016 presidential elec-tion. Every pundit said a Trump win would be very bad initially for the stock market. Most suggested that stocks would go down at least 10 percent. They looked to be right at 2:00 a.m., but by the time the market opened, stocks were actually up. They re-mained up for the next two weeks. So it is very tough to make short-term trading calls.

The allocation process of shares in bank mutual stock offerings is very different from the typical IPO allocation where small investors receive very few shares if any. In bank mutual stock offerings, the size of an investor's share allocation depends on the size of the account he or she has at the bank. The larger his or her deposit at the bank, the more shares he or she will receive in the stock offering. This is done to reward the long-term depositors with the opportunity to become substantial stakeholders in the bank.

It is imperative if a person wants to participate in these offerings that he or she opens an account at these banks with a deposit of at least $5,000 to $10,000. In the 1980s and 1990s, even a small one-hundred-dollar deposit would enable an investor to get full allocations in the offering. But many professional investors started opening accounts at these banks. So the price of poker went up, or in other words, a depositor at the bank now has to have a meaningful deposit to get full share allocation in the stock offering. Depositors also get preferential treatment in the allocation process before borrowers are allowed to participate in these offerings. Therefore, an individual with a car loan will not be given the same buying opportunity that the savings account holder will receive. In my thirty years as a financial adviser, I know of no other investment where a five or ten thousand deposit in a bank can allow an individual investor the opportunity to buy up to $600,000 worth of stock in an IPO.

In 1992, I opened an account for myself and my wife at Home Loan Savings of Fort Wayne. Eighteen months later, on August 14, 1993, it went public. After reading the Peter Lynch article and others on how well these offerings performed, I tried to accumulate as much money as I could to participate in the IPO. I even borrowed money to purchase the maximum shares that I could acquire in the stock offering. This would be one of the only investments I would encourage investors to borrow money to participate in. Other investments have too much inherent risk to use borrowed money and pay interest on that money. When an investor is borrowing money or using margin to invest, he or she must also recoup the interest being paid to the bank.

All investors who participate in these offerings receive an order form and a prospectus from the bank about a month before the offering will take place. On this form, the bank will ask for your account number at the bank and how many shares you want to purchase. This purchase amount can vary from as small as $100,000 up to $600,000. The order form is then sent back to the bank with a check to buy shares in the offering. You then will wait for an underwriting firm such as KBW or Sandler O'Neill, to determine how many shares you will receive in the offering. Many of these offerings are oversubscribed. This means there were more depositors trying to buy shares of stock than were being offered by the bank. The size of your deposit at the bank will determine how many shares you will receive if the offering is oversold. This allocation process to see how many shares a depositor will receive usually takes three weeks after you send your check back to the bank.

Most of these bank mutual offerings begin trading on the NASDAQ stock market. The NASDAQ exchange enables more firms to make a market in the shares after they begin trading. A market maker establishes a bid and an ask for the newly formed company. The bid is what someone is willing to pay for the stock, and the ask is where someone is willing to sell their stock. Most bank conversions typically begin trading at $10 per share. The Home Loan stock I purchased at $10 per share began trading at $12 per share on the opening trade, and within a week it was trading at $14 per share. Some investors may want to take their quick profit in these conversions. This usually occurs during the first week of trading. But after the first week, the volume of trades that occur in the new issue declines dramatically. Most of the investors in these conversions are long-term holders. The local investors want to see their local bank do well over the long term. Bank executives and insiders are also prohibited from selling their shares for a period of at least one year. All of these factors create an upward price movement in the shares of the new bank due to a lack of selling by many investors. Eventually, a larger bank at roughly three times the original offering price bought out Home Loan Savings. After another acquisition, a former Home Loan shareholder is now a holder of Fifth Third Bancorp shares. This takes place often with smaller banks when a larger bank wants to move into the area to gain market share in that city. In 1993, I was thirty-two years old, and in a month I had made $131,000 on my local banks stock offering. The amount I had in my bank deposit was less than $5,000. Not a bad return from a $5,000 savings account! I asked myself, "Where can I find more of these bank investment IPO opportunities?" I would have had a greater return if I had never sold any of my Home Loan shares. If I did not take my profit, I would now be a holder of Fifth Third Bancorp shares. The investment would have grown five times in value more than my original investment. I use buy and hold strategy today when I am involved in a bank conversion. I also try to make these investments in my IRA account so that I can defer the taxes due on any gains. In 1993, I needed to take the gains I made in Home Loan to fund deposits in future banks.

CHAPTER 3

EXPANDING MY OPERATION: WHAT IS A MUTUALLY OWNED BANK?

After the success I had in the Home Loan offering, I wanted to see how I could participate in more mutual bank conversions. It is important to understand what a mutually owned bank is. You may have a local bank in your town, but it may not be a mutual bank where you can participate in a future IPO.

Many small towns may have a bank that was created by a family or group of investors years ago. These banks are typically called private banks. A depositor can become a private shareholder by buying stock directly from the bank. This would only occur when another private shareholder would want to sell his or her shares. The shares typically are priced close to the private bank's book value when sold to new shareholders. As the book value of the private bank increases, so does the value of their shareholders.

A mutual savings bank does not have any current shareholders or owners. The depositors and borrowers are the owners of the bank. If a conversion or IPO takes place, they are the people who can buy stock in the bank and become shareholders. A mutually owned bank has a bank president and officers who make decisions on behalf of the bank. However, until a stock conversion takes place, there are no owners of the bank.

Most of these mutual banks have been around for a number of years; some are over one hundred years old. A mutually owned bank is very similar to the Bailey Building and Loan in Frank Capra's Christmas classic *It's a Wonderful Life.* Recall when Henry F. Potter, the local banker and richest man in town, tries to control the Building and Loan by telling depositors that there is a run on the bank and he will give them fifty cents on the dollar if they turn their shares over to him. If a majority of depositors had given Potter their shares, he would have owned and controlled the Building and Loan. George Bailey then explains how Martha's money is in Sam's house and vice versa. This analogy shows how mutually owned banks work. The depositors and borrowers are sole owners of the bank. The mutual savings banks are the type of institutions to open accounts in to participate in a potential IPO like the Home Loan offering I participated in.

Banks like JP Morgan have shareholders that keep a portion of the bank's profits. These banks have to answer to shareholders, whereas the profits of a mutually owned bank are passed to the depositors. Until a mutual bank converts into a public company, there are no shareholders with whom the bank needs to appease. A mutual bank has no owners, and its sole purpose is to serve the community. JP Morgan needs to make decisions and policies that are in the interest of their shareholders. Mutually owned banks make decisions that will help benefit the local community. The first United States savings bank was designed as a philanthropic concern designed to uplift the poor and working classes. The donors took on positions at the bank as trustees or presidents of the bank. The purpose of creating these banks was to teach the poor the virtues of savings by allowing them to put their money in the bank. The first incorporated mutual savings bank was the Provident Institution for Savings in Boston. Their charter in 1816 was the first government legislation passed in the world to safeguard savings banks.

Mutual savings banks were designed to stimulate savings by individuals. Their main purpose was to protect deposits and make secure investments with these monies. They also provided interest to the depositors on their money. All of the bank profits, except for upkeep costs and salaries for employees, belong to the depositors of the bank. Mutual savings banks have historically made all of their investments in very conservative vehicles. This conservatism allowed mutual savings banks to remain stable throughout the periods of the Great Depression in the 1930s. During this time, many commercial and savings banks went bankrupt from bad and risky investments. The mutual banks, by their conservative nature, were only investing their funds in ultra-safe investments, thus they remained solvent. Excessive leverage is what kills banks in tough times. Leverage is the amount of money a financial institution will borrow to finance their investment portfolio. This is what caused the financial crisis in 2008. Banks like Lehman Brothers and Bear Stearns borrowed excessively to expand their mortgage securities portfolio. Many of the loans were made without proper income verification to people who could not afford the homes they were buying. Some of these banks leveraged their balance sheet assets as high as thirty times what they owned. Leverage or borrowing money only works if the investment goes up in value. If the investments you are borrowing for loses value, it forces banks into a liquidity crisis. This is what happened in 2008, which forced some of these banks into bankruptcy. If not for the government bailout in 2009, many other banks would have filed bankruptcy. These bankruptcies were mainly due to excess leverage.

My main objective in 1993 was to participate in more of these mutual conversions after the success I had with our local savings bank IPO. In 1993, there was no Google or search engine to access facts or information. I went to the local library and researched mutually owned banks. I was able to find a master list of all mutually owned banks in the country. Today these can be found on Google by searching "mutually owned savings banks." It is much easier accessing information than we did with today's advancements in technology.

I also recommend that people interested in this investment thesis subscribe to *SNL Bank and Thrift* updates to stay on top of this industry and the remaining mutual savings banks. This daily publication will provide news on any thrift that may be considering going public. *SNL* will give information on the amount of stock the insiders are buying in each offering. Participating in this investment endeavor will take some time and effort. I recommend creating an Excel spreadsheet to track deposits or purchasing software like Quicken. This will allow you to know when your CDs will mature in case you want add money to the account. This spreadsheet should also include your account number that you will need to input on any order form you may receive in a potential stock offering. By updating your accounts on a spreadsheet, you will have a current value of your deposit which will help ensure your account remains active at the bank. If you do not have activity at the bank over a two-year period, they may send your deposit to the Unclaimed Property division of the state where the bank is located. This would disqualify you from any potential stock offering and force you to go recoup your investment. You would also have to file paperwork to claim your deposit. So, make your deposit accounts become like a side business that you own. Every January you will receive more mail than all of your neighbors combined when all of the 1099 forms come from the various bank accounts you own. But for all these little inconveniences, you will be glad you opened these accounts when a few of them convert and go public.

CHAPTER 4

HISTORY OF THE UNITED STATES BANKING SYSTEM

Henry Ford once said, "It is well enough that people of the nation do not understand our banking and monetary system, for if they did, I believe there would be a revolution before to-morrow morning."

In the mid-1700s, the colonies had no banking system or common currency. While foreign coins and some colonial paper money were in circulation, bartering was the common means of payment. The country chartered the first bank of the United States in 1791. This was the government's first attempt at creating a central bank. The bank had a twenty-year charter, which was not renewed. In 1811, the bank was backed by New York merchants and chartered by the State of New York. Today that bank is known as Citibank.

In the decades to follow, the commercial banking system endured political attacks, economic depressions, and angry mobs. Banking became so deeply seated in the lives of Americans that life without banks today is hard to imagine. Today, almost everyone has a bank account, credit card, loans, or a mortgage.

In the early republic, there were two types of banks: commercial and saving banks. Today, the same bank will perform many different economic functions. They accept deposits, create loans, and offer revolving credit via plastic cards. In the early days of the United States, banking functions were not as integrated. Distinct institutions performed different banking functions. In the early republic, savings banks only maintained time deposits for individual use. Loans to purchase land came directly from the landowner or the government. Today it makes little difference to people whether their money is in a savings bank, a credit agency, or a commercial bank.

Merchants, brokers, and commercial banks conducted currency exchanges, while commercial banks accepted special and demand accounts. They also created deposits by loaning out money that could be drawn on by a check. Commercial banks used loans to issue their own promissory notes payable to the bearer by demand.

The notes of the commercial banks were redeemable in specie. By presenting the note at the bank of issue, the bearer received the note's face value in gold or silver. Merchants back then considered banknotes the equivalent of specie. A bank that could not convert its notes into silver or gold was considered insolvent and lost its charter. Commercial loans were different from today's loans—back then interest was collected upfront. The forms of collateral security were also different from today.

In 1775, there were no commercial banks in Britain's rebellious American colonies. The commercial Bank of England was at the time almost a century old; however, few colonists had any dealings with it or Britain's enormously funded debt. There did exist colonial institutions, both private and public, that went by the name of a bank. Most of these institutions were so different from commercial banks that Alexander Hamilton and other founding financiers proposed the Bank of North America in 1781 and the Bank of New York in 1784. Every aspect of banking was discussed repeatedly and in great detail.

Many other key moments in the history of the United States banking system occurred in the 1900s. In 1900 the United States adopted the gold standard. United States currency was equal and exchangeable for gold during these years. In 1913, the Federal Reserve System was created. Before the Federal Reserve was founded, the nation was plagued by financial crises. These would lead to people going to the bank to withdraw their deposits. The failure of one bank would then have a domino effect in which people would withdraw their money from even solvent banks. This created many bank runs during this time period. Banks needed a source of emergency reserves to prevent these panics and resulting runs from driving them out of business. The Federal Reserve was created to foster a sound banking system and healthy economy.

In 1929 the stock market crashed, and the Great Depression began. The growth of the roaring 1920s had caused excess speculation by the end of the decade. Many investors were buying stocks on margin to bid up share prices to extreme levels. Excess leverage was also the cause of the recent financial crisis in 2009. In 1933, the Federal Deposit Insurance Corporation (FDIC) was established to protect depositors against a bank failure. Also in 1933, the United States ended the domestic gold standard. U.S. currency is no longer equal to or exchangeable for gold.

In 1958, Bank of America issued the first credit card, now called the Visa card. In 1969, the first ATM began operation in New York, allowing individuals immediate access to cash. By 1997, more than 160,000 ATMs were operating across the United States. In 2003 a new twenty-dollar bill was issued, followed by a new fifty-dollar bill in 2004. These were created to improve security and stop counterfeiting.

In late 2007, a global financial crisis began, triggered by a liquidity shortfall in the United States banking system.

In 2008, the Economic Stabilization Act was passed to allow the US government to buy nonliquid assets from banks and other financial institutions. In 2010, the Dodd-Frank Bill became federal law. This was designed to improve accountability and transparency in the financial system. Finally, in 2011, for the first time in history, the United States had its credit rating lowered from AAA to AA+, thus removing the United States from the global list of risk-free borrowers.

CHAPTER 5

WHY DOES A MUTUAL SAVINGS BANK GO PUBLIC?

A mutual company is owned and governed by its members instead of being owned by public and private shareholders. Over the past few decades, a number of mutuals have converted to a stock form of ownership. There are a variety of reasons a bank would want to convert to a public company. The most common is that bank needs capital to expand its footprint. Some of these banks want to open new branches, whereas others may use the newfound capital to acquire other banks. Some retiring presidents may use the stock conversion strategy as their exit strategy. Many of the banks that have converted over the past few years have had some financial difficulties and in some cases needed to get capital to bolster their balance sheets. Even though many of these mutual banks had balance sheet issues, they still had positive returns for their depositors upon converting.

On October 1, 2014, Macon Bank of North Carolina went public at $10 per share. The bank had a very high amount of non-performing assets (NPA). Non-performing assets are loans that the bank is not collecting payments on. The bank eventually writes off many of these bad loans. Most savings banks have about 1 to 2 percent of their loans classified as NPAs. Macon Bank had 10 percent of their loans coded as NPAs. When I received the prospectus on the Macon offering, I was worried that these loans that had created losses at the bank for the prior three years might reduce the number of depositors who would want to invest in conversion. But six months earlier I had an analyst tell me not to participate in a Richmond, Indiana, conversion that took place. I followed her advice and did not invest in the West End Bank conversion. The shares of the West End offering soon began trading at a price of $14 per share or a 40 percent gain. I was very disappointed and promised myself that I would always participate in any future offering that I was given the opportunity to invest in. The Macon Bank conversion, even with 10 percent of their loans classified as non-performing, still had a significant increase in their stock price upon conversion. The shares of Macon Bank began trading at $13 per share and today trades at $19 per share, a 90 percent return for depositors or investors who held on to their shares of stock over a two-year period.

Some of the smaller mutual banks with assets of less than 100 million try to gain efficiencies and cost savings by merging with a mutual bank of similar size. Many banks in Massachusetts have done this lately. Holbrook Cooperative Bank and Abington Bank recently announced they are merging together. The two banks were almost forced to merge due to rising regulatory costs facing small local banks. They will be able to reduce expenses by combining their information technology and back office areas. When two mutual banks merge, there is no IPO event that takes place. But down the road the combined new company may decide to convert and go public. As a larger bank with more assets, they become a more attractive potential IPO.

The number of banks currently looking to convert is much lower than in past years. Mutual banks converted regularly in the 1990s and the first decade of 2000. During this time period, banks converted to public ownership at a rate of about seventeen per year. Only seven mutual banks converted to become a publically traded company in 2016. Parts of the Dodd-Frank Bill have made it much costlier for smaller banks to convert and become a public company. Increased regulations and increasing compliance costs have dramatically slowed the pace of mutual bank conversions. There is hope that under the Trump administration some of these strict regulations on small banks will be relaxed. Fewer regulations will help the smaller banks to reduce costs and become more profitable. In a less regulated environment, maybe more mutual banks will decide to convert and go public. This would create more investment opportunities for depositors.

Since 2010, there have been about fifty mutual bank conversions. However, not every mutual bank will convert into a stock-owned company. Some bank presidents are opposed to going public because it does not fit the membership style of the depositors owning the bank, and they do not want to have to deal with the concern of public shareholders. These banks take a very keen interest in the needs and wants of the community. Many of these banks have been mutually owned for over a hundred years. They enjoy the autonomy of existing for the causes of their small towns. Until the officers of these banks change their agenda, they will remain mutually owned.

If a mutual bank does decide to issue stock, there are two types of conversions that a savings bank can undertake. One is called a standard conversion, and the other is a mutual holding company (MHC) conversion. In a standard conversion, all share ownership of the membership is transferred to public shareholders. They will be a fully public company like all other companies, such as General Electric or Wells Fargo. There will be a board of directors that will oversee the company, but full ownership will belong to the public shareholders.

The MHC conversion allows the bank to convert in steps. The bank will sell a minority stake to the public or depositors and keep ownership of the majority shares in-house. Then at a later date, the bank can do a second-step offering to the public to become a fully converted public company. This option allows the bank's management to maintain control over all decisions at the bank. The minority shareholders cannot refute any of the bank's decisions.

Shares of partially converted mutually owned banks can be purchased on the open market like any other stock. The key is to look for banks trading below their book value. Most of these conversions are priced in 35 to 50 percent below the bank's current book value. This is done to ensure significant interest for their shares in the open market. Many mutual funds and professional investors will buy these banks even after they convert and are trading in the open market.

After a mutual bank conversion takes place, a larger bank can buy it. This, however, can only take place after three years of being a public company. This gives investors or depositors another opportunity to gain even larger returns on their initial investment. However, stock buybacks by the bank can begin one year after the conversion takes place. A stock buyback is when an issuer (the bank) purchases its own shares in the open market. Many companies buy back their own stock. It is a sign that management believes their company shares may be undervalued or are optimistic of the future. This company buyback of shares can create an upward push to the stock price of the newly converted bank.

About one-third of all converted mutual banks end up being acquired by a larger bank. The average time before a merger takes place is almost two years after the three years post conversion moratorium expires. Danvers Bancorp in Massachusetts was a bank IPO in which I participated in 2008. It was acquired just ten days after their three-year anniversary of being a public company. Danvers Bancorp was bought out by People's United Financial at a price of 160 percent of book value. Not a bad return for depositors that bought the stock at 60 percent below book value three years earlier. The acquisition option is the final and most lucrative outcome for the savings bank investment thesis.

CHAPTER 6

WHERE ARE THESE MUTUAL SAVINGS BANKS, AND HOW DO I INVEST IN THEM?

I n 1775, all the British colonies were on the East Coast. This is where the original thirteen states were established. Therefore, it is no surprise that most of the mutually owned savings banks are located in the northeastern part of the country. The majority of these mutually owned savings banks reside in Massachusetts. Today 111 of the remaining 577 mutual banks are located in the state of Massachusetts. If you live specifically in the Boston area, you have a phenomenal investment opportunity. All of the little towns, from Dedham, Peabody, and Wellesley, have or had their own local savings bank. They were created many years ago for their local town's interests and owned by their depositors. Many of these banks had names like Ben Franklin Savings, depicting the time and individuals of the late 1700s where they issued their own banknotes. Since the 1970s, when the industry was deregulated, thousands of mutual savings banks have been converted to stock ownership companies, raising more than $40 billion. These conversions have often resulted in large financial rewards for top bank executives.

The first incorporated U.S. mutual savings bank was the Provident Institution for Savings in Boston. Its 1816 charter was the first government legislation in the world to safeguard savings banks. Wealthy individuals tried to teach the lower income classes the virtues of thrift and self-reliance by allowing them the security to save their money. This is how these savings banks were created.

Very few mutual banks are located in the western part of the country. This is due to the fact that these states were all established in later years. I have listed below a summary of the remaining mutually owned banks in the United States.

Here's the most recent list of mutual institutions and stock institutions owned by mutual holding companies from the Federal Deposit Insurance Corporation's website:

Mount McKinley Bank — Fairbanks, AK
Cullman Savings Bank — Cullman, AL
First Federal Savings and Loan Association
of San Rafael — San Rafael, CA

San Luis Valley Federal Bank — Alamosa, CO
Rio Grande savings and loan association — Monte Vista, CO
Century Savings and Loan Association — Trinidad, CO
Gunnison savings and loan association — Gunnison, CO
Del Norte Bank — Del Norte, CO
Windsor Federal Savings and Loan Association — Windsor, CT
Union Savings Bank — Danbury, CT
The Guilford Savings Bank — Guilford, CT
Ion Bank — Naugatuck, CT
Newtown Savings Bank — Newtown, CT
Dime Bank — Norwich, CT
First County Bank — Stamford, CT
Litchfield Bancorp — Litchfield, CT
Fairfield County Bank — Ridgefield, CT
Collinsville Savings Society — Canton, CT
Stafford Savings Bank — Stafford Spring, CT
Northwest Community Bank — Winsted, CT
Jewett City Savings Bank — Jewett City, CT
Chelsea Groton Bank — Norwich, CT
Putnam Bank — Putnam, CT
Thomaston Savings Bank — Thomaston, CT
Savings Bank of Danbury — Danbury, CT
The Milford Bank — Milford, CT
The Torrington Savings Bank — Torrington, CT
Essex Savings Bank — Essex, CT
Liberty Bank — Middletown, CT

Eastern Savings Bank — Norwich, CT
Artisans' Bank — Wilmington, DE
First Federal Bank of Florida — Lake City, FL
Elberton Federal Savings and Loan
Association — Elberton, GA
First Federal Savings and Loan
Association of Valdosta --- Valdosta, GA
Thomas County Federal Savings and
Loan Association — Thomasville, GA
Newton Federal Bank — Covington, GA
Family Bank — Pelham, GA
Vidalia Federal Savings Bank — Vidalia, GA
WCF Financial Bank — Webster City, IA
Interstate Federal Savings and Loan
Association of McGregor — McGregor, IA
First Federal Savings Bank of
Twin Falls — Twin Falls, ID
Collinsville Building and Loan
Association — Collinsville, IL
Nokomis Savings Bank — Nokomis, IL
De Witt Savings Bank — Clinton, IL
North Shore Trust and Savings —
Waukegan, IL
North Side Federal Savings and Loan
Association of Chicago — Chicago, IL
Flora Savings Bank — Flora, IL
Security Bank — Springfield, IL
Sterling Federal Bank, FSB — Sterling, IL
Union Federal Savings and Loan
Association — Kewanee, IL

Home Federal Savings and Loan Association
of Collinsville — Collinsville, IL
Central Federal Savings and Loan
Association of Chicago — Chicago, IL
Ottawa Savings Bank — Ottawa, IL
Prospect Federal Savings Bank — Worth, IL
First Federal Savings and Loan Association
of Central Illinois — Shelbyville, IL
Mutual Federal Bank — Chicago, IL
Ben Franklin Bank of Illinois —
Arlington Heights, IL
Eureka Savings Bank — La Salle, IL
Central Federal Savings and Loan
Association — Cicero, IL
Pulaski Savings Bank — Chicago, IL
First Savings Bank — Danville, IL
Nashville Savings Bank — Nashville, IL
First Savings Bank of Hegewisch —
Chicago, IL
Hoyne Savings Bank — Chicago, IL
Loomis Federal Savings and Loan
Association — Chicago, IL
Community Savings Bank — Chicago, IL
First Federal Savings Bank — Ottawa, IL
Security Savings Bank — Monmouth, IL
Lisle Savings Bank — Lisle, IL
Guardian Savings Bank — Granite City, IL
Harvard Savings Bank — Harvard, IL
Liberty Bank for Savings — Chicago, IL
Union Savings Bank — Freeport, IL

Washington Savings Bank — Effingham, IL
Peru Federal Savings Bank — Peru, IL
Illinois-Service Federal Savings and
Loan Association — Chicago, IL
Beardstown Saving's — Beardstown, IL
First FSB of Mascoutah — Mascoutah, IL
First Savanna Savings Bank — Savanna, IL
Streator Home Savings Bank — Streator, IL
Wabash Savings Bank — Mount Carmel, IL
North County Savings Bank — Red Bud, IL
Marion County Savings Bank — Salem, IL
Milford Building and Loan
Association — Milford, IL
First Federal Savings Bank of
Angola — Angola, IN
Lake Federal Bank, FSB — Hammond, IN
Scottsburg Building and Loan
Association — Scottsburg, IN
Kentland Federal Savings and Loan
Association — Kentland, IN
First Federal Savings Bank of
Washington — Washington, IN
Farmers and Mechanics Federal Savings
and Loan Association — Bloomfield, IN
Terre Haute Savings Bank — Terre Haute, IN
First Bank Richmond, National
Association — Richmond, IN
Bedford Federal Savings Bank — Bedford, IN
Security Federal Savings Bank —
Logansport, IN

Home Bank SB — Martinsville, IN
Union Savings and Loan
Association — Connersville, IN
First Federal Savings and Loan Association
of Greensburg — Greenburg, IN
Peoples Savings and Loan Association of
Monticello Indiana — Monticello, IN
Boonville Federal Savings
Bank — Boonville, IN
Mid-Southern Savings Bank,
FSB — Salem, IN
Lyons Federal Bank — Lyons, KS
Home Savings Bank — Chanute, KS
Argentine Federal Savings —
Kansas City, KS
The Liberty Savings Association,
FSA — Fort Scott, KS
First Federal Savings and Loan Association
of Wakeeney — Wakeeney, KS
Inter-State Federal Savings and Loan
Association of Kansas City — Kansas City, KS
Citizens Savings and Loan Association,
FSB — Leavenworth, KS
Mutual Savings Association,
FSA — Leavenworth, KS
Citizens Federal Savings and Loan
Association — Covington, KY
Kentucky Federal Savings and Loan
Association — Covington, KY
Carrollton Federal Bank — Carrollton, KY

First Federal Savings Bank of
Kentucky — Frankfort, KY
First Federal Savings and Loan
Association — Morehead, KY
Blue Grass Federal Savings and
Loan Association — Paris, KY
Home Savings Bank, FSB — Ludlow, KY
First Federal Savings and Loan
Association — Hazard, KY
St Landry Homestead Federal
Savings Bank — Opelousas, LA
Heritage Bank of St Tammany —
Covington, LA
Citizens Savings Bank — Bogalusa, LA
Mutual Savings and Loan
Association — Metairie, LA
Union Savings and Loan Association —
New Orleans, LA
Fifth District Savings Bank —
New Orleans, LA
Fidelity Bank — New Orleans, LA
Eureka Homestead — Metairie, LA
First Federal Bank of Louisiana —
Lake Charles, LA
Rayne Building and Loan
Association — Rayne, LA
Abbeville Building & Loan (A State-
Chartered Savings Bank) --- Abbeville, LA
Rollstone Bank & Trust — Fitchburg, MA
Cambridge Savings Bank — Cambridge, MA
Millbury Savings Bank — Millbury, MA

Fall River Five Cents Savings
Bank — Fall River, MA
The Cape Cod Five Cents Savings
Bank — Harwich Port, MA
Florence Savings Bank — Florence, MA
Salem Five Cents Savings Bank — Salem, MA
Watertown Savings Bank — Watertown, MA
Southbridge Savings Bank —
Southbridge, MA
Dedham Institution for
Savings — Dedham, MA
Bristol County Savings Bank — Taunton, MA
Country Bank for Savings — Ware, MA
The Village Bank — Auburndale, MA
The Pittsfield Cooperative
Bank — Pittsfield, MA
Mutual One Bank — Framingham, MA
Greenfield Cooperative Bank —
Greenfield, MA
Haverhill Bank — Haverhill, MA
Everett Co-operative Bank — Everett, MA
Mansfield Co-operative Bank —
Mansfield, MA
Canton Co-operative Bank — Canton, MA
Fidelity Co-operative Bank — Fitchburg, MA
Equitable Co-operative Bank — Lynn, MA
Savers Co-operative Bank —
Southbridge, MA
Needham Bank — Needham, MA
North Shore Bank — Peabody, MA
Walpole Co-operative Bank — Walpole, MA

Melrose Cooperative Bank —Melrose, MA
Methuen Cooperative Bank — Methuen, MA
Stoughton Co-operative Bank — Stoughton, MA
Wakefield Co-operative Bank — Wakefield, MA
The Cooperative Bank of Cape Cod — Yarmouth Port, MA
Hometown Bank, A Cooperative Bank — Oxford, MA
Bank Gloucester — Gloucester, MA
Abington Bank — Abington, MA
Bank of Easton — North Easton, MA
Norwood Cooperative Bank — Norwood, MA
Colonial Co-operative Bank — Gardner, MA
Stoneham Bank — Stoneham, MA
North Cambridge Co-operative Bank — Cambridge, MA
The Braintree Cooperative Bank — Braintree, MA
Coastal Heritage Bank — Weymouth, MA
Wrentham Cooperative Bank — Wrentham, MA
Weymouth Bank — East Weymouth, MA
Holbrook Cooperative Bank — Holbrook, MA
Beverly Bank — Beverly, MA
Charles River Bank — Medway, MA
Avon Co-operative Bank — Avon, MA
Reading Cooperative Bank — Reading, MA

Mechanics Cooperative
Bank — Taunton, MA
The Cooperative Bank — Roslindale, MA
Winchester Co-operative Bank —
Winchester, MA
Dean Bank — Franklin, MA
Foxboro Federal Savings — Foxboro, MA
Winter Hill Bank, FSB — Somerville, MA
Middlesex Federal Savings,
FA — Somerville, MA
Colonial Federal Savings Bank — Quincy, MA
Mutual Bank — Whitman, MA
Milford Federal Savings and Loan
Association — Milford, MA
Commonwealth Cooperative
Bank — Hyde Park, MA
Family Federal Savings, FA — Fitchburg, MA
Eastern Bank — Boston, MA
Lee Bank — Lee, MA
Harbor One Bank — Brockton, MA
Adams Community Bank — Adams, MA
The Provident Bank — Amesbury, MA
Athol Savings Bank — Athol, MA
North Middlesex Savings Bank — Ayer, MA
Barre Savings Bank — Barre, MA
Bridgewater Savings Bank — Raynham, MA
East Cambridge Savings Bank —
Cambridge, MA
The Bank of Canton — Canton, MA
Clinton Savings Bank — Clinton, MA

Middlesex Savings Bank — Natick, MA
Easthampton Savings Bank —
Easthampton, MA
Martha's Vineyard Savings
Bank — Edgartown, MA
Eagle Bank — Everett, MA
Bay Coast Bank — Fall River, MA
Cape Ann Savings Bank — Gloucester, MA
Greenfield Savings Bank — Greenfield, MA
Pentucket Bank — Haverhill, MA
Peoples Bank — Holyoke, MA
Avidia Bank — Hudson, MA
The Lowell Five Cent Savings
Bank — Lowell, MA
Washington Savings Bank — Lowell, MA
Marblehead Bank — Marblehead, MA
Marlborough Savings Bank —
Marlborough, MA
Monson Savings Bank — Monson, MA
Institution for Savings in Newburyport
and Its Vicinity — Newburyport, MA
Newburyport Five Cents Savings
Bank — Newburyport, MA
Mountain One Bank — North Adams, MA
North Brookfield Savings Bank —
North Brookfield, MA
North Easton Savings Bank —
South Easton, MA
Seamen's Bank — Provincetown, MA
Randolph Savings Bank — Randolph, MA

Spencer Savings Bank — Spencer, MA
UniBank for Savings — Whitinsville, MA
The Savings Bank — Wakefield, MA
Webster Five Cents Savings
Bank — Webster, MA
South Shore Bank — South Weymouth, MA
Winchester Savings Bank —
Winchester, MA
Bay State Savings Bank — Worcester, MA
Saint Casmir's Savings Bank —
Baltimore, MD
Madison Bank of Maryland —
Forest Hill, MD
The Glen Burnie Mutual Savings
Bank — Glen Burnie, MD
Chesapeake Bank of Maryland —
Parkville, MD
Arundel Federal Savings Bank —
Glen Burnie, MD
Rosedale Federal Savings and Loan
Association — Nottingham, MD
Kopernik Bank — Baltimore, MD
Midstate Community Bank — Baltimore, MD
Liberty Bank of Maryland — Baltimore, MD
First Shore Federal Savings and Loan
Association — Salisbury, MD
Jarrettsville Federal Savings and Loan
Association — Jarrettsville, MD
North Arundel Savings Bank —
Pasadena, MD

Homewood Federal Savings
Bank — Baltimore, MD
Bay-Vanguard Federal Savings
Bank — Baltimore, MD
Rockland Savings Bank,
FSB — Rockland, ME
Kennebunk Savings Bank — Kennebunk, ME
Sanford Institution for
Savings — Sanford, ME
Mechanics' Savings Bank — Auburn, ME
Norway Savings Bank — Norway, ME
Biddeford Savings Bank — Biddeford, ME
Saco & Biddeford Savings
Institution — Saco, ME
Gorham Savings Bank — Gorham, ME
Bath Savings Institution — Bath, ME
Androscoggin Savings Bank — Lewiston, ME
Bangor Savings Bank — Bangor, ME
Macias Savings Bank — Machias, ME
Skowhegan Savings Bank — Skowhegan, ME
Franklin Savings Bank — Farmington, ME
Kennebec Savings Bank — Augusta, ME
Auburn Savings Bank, FSB — Auburn, ME
First Federal Savings and Loan
Association of Bath — Bath, ME
Kennebec Federal Savings and Loan
Association of Waterville — Waterville, ME
Aroostook County Federal Savings and
Loan Association — Caribou, ME
Bar Harbor Savings and Loan
Association — Bar Harbor, ME

Homestead Savings Bank — Albion, MI
Eaton Federal Savings Bank — Charlotte, MI
Dearborn Federal Savings
Bank — Dearborn, MI
Lake City Federal Bank — Lake City, MN
Worthington Federal Savings Bank,
FSB — Worthington, MN
Brainerd Savings and Loan Association,
A Federal Association — Brainerd, MN
Jackson Federal Savings and Loan
Association — Jackson, MN
Think Mutual Bank — Rochester, MN
Home Savings and Loan Association,
FA — Norborne, MO
Home Savings Bank — Jefferson City, MO
West Plains Savings and Loan
Association — West Plains, MO
Ozarks Federal Savings and Loan
Association — Farmington, MO
First Federal Bank, FSB — Kansas City, MO
Systematic Savings Bank — Springfield, MO
Mississippi County Savings and Loan
Association — Charleston, MO
Central Federal Savings and Loan
Association of Rolla — Rolla, MO
Carroll County Savings and Loan
Association — Carrolton, MO
American Loan and Savings
Association — Hannibal, MO
Amory Federal Savings and Loan
Association — Amory, MS

First Federal Savings and Loan
Association — Aberdeen, MS
First Federal Savings and Loan
Association — Pascagoula, MS
Pioneer Federal Savings and Loan
Association — Deer Lodge, MT
Piedmont Federal Savings Bank —
Winston Salem, NC
Wake Forest Federal Savings and Loan
Association — Wake Forest, NC
Black Mountain Savings Bank,
SSB — Black Mountain, NC
Belmont Federal Savings and Loan
Association — Belmont, NC
Roanoke Rapids Savings Bank,
SSB — Roanoke Rapids, NC
Roxboro Savings Bank, SSB — Roxboro, NC
Tarboro Savings Bank, SSB — Tarboro, NC
Roanoke Valley Savings Bank,
SSB — Roanoke Rapids, NC
First Federal Savings Bank of
Lincolnton — Lincolnton, NC
Taylorsville Savings Bank,
SSB — Taylorsville, NC
First Savings and Loan
Association — Mebane, NC
Morganton Savings Bank,
SSB — Morganton, NC
Life Store Bank — West Jefferson, NC
Jackson Savings Bank, SSB — Sylva, NC
Hertford Savings Bank, SSB — Hertford, NC

Gate City Bank — Fargo, ND
Sidney Federal Savings and Loan
Association — Sidney, NE
Home Federal Savings and Loan Association
of Grand Island — Grand Island, NE
Lincoln FSB of Nebraska — Lincoln, NE
Tecumseh Federal Bank — Tecumseh, NE
Meredith Village Savings
Bank — Meredith, NH
Piscataqua Savings Bank — Portsmouth, NH
Franklin Savings Bank — Franklin, NH
Merrimack County Savings
Bank — Concord, NH
Bank of New Hampshire — Laconia, NH
Mascoma Savings Bank — Lebanon, NH
Sugar River Bank — Newport, NH
Savings Bank of Walpole — Walpole, NH
Claremont Savings Bank — Claremont, NH
Profile Bank — Rochester, NH
Salem Cooperative Bank — Salem, NH
Federal Savings Bank — Dover, NH
Union County Savings Bank — Elizabeth, NJ
RSI Bank — Rahway, NJ
Audubon Savings Bank — Audubon, NJ
Haddon Savings Bank —
Haddon Heights, NJ
Roselle Savings Bank — Roselle, NJ
GSL Savings Bank — Guttenberg, NJ
Glen Rock Savings Bank — Glen Rock, NJ
Somerset Savings Bank, SLA —
Bound Brook, NJ

Sturdy Savings Bank — Stone Harbor, NJ
Crest Savings Bank — Wildwood, NJ
Columbia Bank — Fair Lawn, NJ
Lincoln Park Savings Bank —
Lincoln Park, NJ
United Roosevelt Savings
Bank — Carteret, NJ
Haven Savings Bank — Hoboken, NJ
Boiling Springs Savings Bank —
Rutherford, NJ
Lusitania Savings Bank — Newark, NJ
Fairport Savings Bank — Fairport, NY
Schuyler Savings Bank — Kearney, NJ
Spencer Savings Bank, SLA —
Elmwood Park, NJ
Metuchen Savings Bank — Metuchen, NJ
Monroe Savings Bank — Williamstown, NJ
Gibraltar Bank — Oak Ridge, NJ
NVE Bank — Englewood, NJ
Millville Savings and Loan
Association — Millville, NJ
Magyar Bank — New Brunswick, NJ
Wawel Bank — Wallington, NJ
Bogota Savings Bank — BOGOTA, NJ
1st Bank of Sea Isle City — Sea Isle City, NJ
Franklin Bank — Pilesgrove, NJ
Century Savings Bank — Vineland, NJ
Manasquan Bank — Manasquan, NJ
Freehold Savings Bank — Freehold, NJ
Tucumcari Federal Savings and Loan
Association — Tucumcari, NM
BANK 34 — Alamogordo, NM

Massena Savings and Loan — Massena, NY
Lake Shore Savings Bank — Dunkirk, NY
Pioneer Savings Bank — Troy, NY
The Bank of Greene County — Catskill, NY
Fulton Savings Bank — Fulton, NY
Rondout Savings Bank — Kingston, NY
Ulster Savings Bank — Kingston, NY
Walden Savings Bank — Montgomery, NY
Watertown Savings Bank — Watertown, NY
PCSB Bank — Brewster, NY
Ridgewood Savings Bank — Ridgewood, NY
The North Country Savings
Bank — Canton, NY
Rhinebeck Bank — Rhinebeck, NY
Sawyer Savings Bank — Saugerties, NY
Generations Bank — Seneca Falls, NY
Hometown Bank of the Hudson
Valley — Walden, NY
First Federal Savings of Middletown —
Middletown, NY
Maple City Savings Bank, FSB —
Hornell, NY
Wallkill Valley Federal Savings and
Loan Association — Wallkill, NY
Carthage Federal Savings and Loan
Association — Carthage, NY
North East Community Bank —
White Plains, NY
Seneca Federal Savings and Loan
Association — Baldwinsville, NY
Cross County Savings Bank —
Middle Village, NY

Maspeth Federal Savings and Loan
Association — Maspeth, NY
Greene County Commercial
Bank — Catskill, NY
Geddes Federal Savings and Loan
Association — Syracuse, NY
Medina Savings and Loan
Association — Medina, NY
Governor Savings and Loan
Association — Gouverneur, NY
Ponce De Leon Federal Bank — Bronx, NY
First Federal Bank of Ohio — Galion, OH
Fairfield Federal Savings and Loan
Association of Lancaster — Lancaster, OH
Greenville Federal — Greenville, OH
Community Savings — Caldwell, OH
Citizens Federal Savings and Loan
Association — Bellefontaine, OH
The Covington Savings and Loan
Association — Covington, OH
The Harrison Building and Loan
Association — Harrison, OH
The Cincinnatus Savings & Loan
Co. — Cincinnati, OH
Warsaw Federal Savings and Loan
Association — Cincinnati, OH
Cincinnati Federal — Cincinnati, OH
Belmont Savings Bank — Bellaire, OH
Liberty Bank — Ironton, OH
Valley Central Bank — Reading, OH

The Brookville Building and Savings
Association — Brookville, OH

Conneaut Savings Bank — Conneaut, OH

First Federal Savings and Loan
Association — Centerburg, OH

First Federal Savings and Loan
Association — Newark, OH

First Federal Savings and Loan Association
of Van Wert — Van Wert, OH

New Carlisle Federal Savings
Bank — New Carlisle, OH

Ripley Federal Savings Bank — Ripley, OH

First Federal Savings and Loan
Association — Delta, OH

First Federal Savings and Loan
Association — Lakewood, OH

Van Wert Federal Savings
Bank — Van Wert, OH

Fidelity Federal Savings and Loan
Association of Delaware — Delaware, OH

The Home Savings and Loan Company
of Kenton, Ohio — Kenton, OH

Monroe Federal Savings and Loan
Association — Tipp City, OH

Southern Hills Community
Bank — Leesburg, OH

Peoples Savings and Loan
Company — Bucyrus, OH

First Federal Savings and Loan
Association of Lorain — Lorain, OH

American Savings Bank — Middletown, OH
The Equitable Savings and Loan
Company — Cadiz, OH
The Peoples Savings Bank — Urbana, OH
Eagle Savings Bank — Cincinnati, OH
Third Federal Savings and Loan Association
of Cleveland — Cleveland, OH
Home Savings Bank of Wapakoneta —
Wapakoneta, OH
Mercer Savings Bank — Celina, OH
Peoples First Savings Bank — Mason, OH
Belpre Savings Bank — Belpre, OH
The Peoples Savings and Loan
Company — West Liberty, OH
The Wilmington Savings Bank —
Wilmington, OH
Community Savings Bank — Bethel, OH
Miami Savings Bank — Miamitown, OH
Adams County Building and Loan
Company — West Union, OH
New Foundation Savings
Bank — Cincinnati, OH
Galion Building and Loan
Bank — Galion, OH
Liberty FSB — Enid, OK
Fairview Savings and Loan
Association — Fairview, OK
Evergreen Federal Savings and Loan
Association — Grants Pass, OR
First Federal Savings and Loan Association
of McMinnville --- McMinnville, OR

Port Richmond Savings — Philadelphia, PA
Slovenian Savings and Loan Association
of Canonsburg — Strabane, PA
Altoona First Savings Bank — Altoona, PA
Indiana First Savings Bank — Indiana, PA
William Penn Bank — Levittown, PA
Progressive-Home Federal Savings and
Loan Association — Pittsburgh, PA
Brentwood Bank — Bethel Park, PA
Mifflin County Savings Bank —
Lewistown, PA
Milton Savings Bank — Milton, PA
Ambler Savings Bank — Ambler, PA
First Federal Savings and Loan Association
of Greene Co. — Waynesburg, PA
Sharon Savings Bank — Darby, PA
United Savings Bank — Philadelphia, PA
Iron Workers Savings Bank — Aston, PA
County Savings Bank — Essington, PA
Washington Savings Bank — Philadelphia, PA
Compass Savings Bank — Wilmerding, PA
Armstrong County Building and
Loan Association — Ford City, PA
Washington Financial Bank —
Washington, PA
Second Federal Savings and Loan
Association of Philadelphia —
Philadelphia, PA
CFSBANK — Charleroi, PA
Union Building and Loan Savings
Bank — West Bridgewater, PA

Phoenixville Federal Bank and
Trust — Phoenixville, PA
Huntingdon Savings Bank —
Huntingdon, PA
Coatesville Savings Bank — Coatesville, PA
Reliance Savings Bank — Altoona, PA
Penn Crest Bank — Altoona, PA
Investment Savings Bank — Altoona, PA
Sewickley Savings Bank — Sewickley, PA
Hatboro Federal Savings, FA — Hatboro, PA
Penn Community Bank — Perkasie, PA
Slovak Savings Bank — Pittsburgh, PA
Huntingdon Valley Bank —
Huntington Valley, PA
Marquette Savings Bank — Erie, PA
Westmoreland Federal Savings and
Loan Association — Latrobe, PA
Greenville Savings Bank — Greenville, PA
Fidelity Savings and Loan Association
of Bucks Co. — Bristol, PA
Citizens Savings Bank — Clarks Summit, PA
Slovenian Savings and Loan Association of
Franklin-Conemaugh — Conemaugh, PA
Dollar Bank, Federal Savings
Bank — Pittsburgh, PA
Tioga-Franklin Savings Bank —
Philadelphia, PA
Bally Savings Bank — Bally, PA
Farmers Building and Savings
Bank — Rochester, PA

Chilton Hills Savings Bank —
Abington, PA
Centreville Savings Bank — West Warwick, RI
Bank of Newport — Newport, RI
First Piedmont Federal Savings and Loan
Association of Gaffney — Gaffney, SC
Woodruff Federal Savings and Loan
Association — Woodruff, SC
Kingstree Federal Savings and Loan
Association — Kingstree, SC
Pee Dee Federal Savings Bank — Marion, SC
Mutual Savings Bank — Hartsville, SC
Oconee Federal Savings and Loan
Association — Seneca, SC
Abbeville First Bank, SSB — Abbeville, SC
Spratt Savings and Loan
Association — Chester, SC
First Federal of South Carolina,
FSB — Walterboro, SC
Home Federal Savings and Loan
Association — Bamberg, SC
Citizens Building and Loan, SSB — Greer, SC
Lawrenceburg Federal Bank —
Lawrenceburg, TN
Home Federal Bank of
Tennessee — Knoxville, TN
Elizabethton Federal Savings
Bank — Elizabethton, TN
Greeneville Federal Bank,
FSB — Greeneville, TN

Highland Federal Savings and Loan
Association — Crossville, TN
Volunteer Federal Savings
Bank — Madisonville, TN
First Federal Community
Bank, SSB — Paris, TX
Trust Texas Bank, SSB — Cuero, TX
Mineola Community Bank,
SSB — Mineola, TX
Dalhart Federal Savings & Loan
Association, SSB — Dalhart, TX
Henderson Federal Savings
Bank — Henderson, TX
Martinsville First Savings Bank —
Martinsville, VA
Bank @LANTEC — Virginia Beach, VA
Passumpsic Savings Bank —
Saint Johnsbury, VT
Wells River Savings Bank — Wells River, VT
Northfield Savings Bank — Northfield, VT
The Brattleboro Savings and Loan
Association — Brattleboro, VT
The Bank of Bennington — Bennington, VT
Yakima Federal Savings and Loan
Association — Yakima, WA
Raymond Federal Bank — Raymond, WA
First Federal Savings and Loan Association
of Port Angeles — Port Angeles, WA
Olympia Federal Savings and Loan
Association — Olympia, WA

1st Security Bank of Washington —
Mountlake Terra, WA
Columbia Savings and Loan
Association — Milwaukee, WI
Forward Financial Bank — Marshfield, WI
The Equitable Bank, SSB — Wauwatosa, WI
North Shore Bank, FSB — Brookfield, WI
Superior Savings Bank — Superior, WI
Ladysmith Federal Savings and Loan
Association — Ladysmith, WI
PyraMax Bank, FSB — Greenfield, WI
Fox Valley Savings Bank — Fond Du Lac, WI
Cumberland Federal Bank,
FSB — Cumberland, WI
Time Federal Savings Bank — Medford, WI
Great Midwest Bank, SSB — Brookfield, WI
Paper City Savings Association —
Wisconsin Rapid, WI
Key Savings Bank — Wisconsin Rapid, WI
Marathon Savings Bank — Wausau, WI
Guaranty Bank — Milwaukee, WI
Merrill Federal Savings and Loan
Association — Merrill, WI
East Wisconsin Savings Bank,
SA — Kaukauna, WI
First Federal Bank of Wisconsin —
Waukesha, WI
Tomahawk Community Bank
SSB — Tomahawk, WI
Mayville Savings Bank — Mayville, WI

Huntington Federal Savings Bank —
Huntington, WV
Hancock County Savings Bank,
FSB — Chester, WV
First Federal Savings & Loan Association
of Ravenswood — Ravenswood, WV
Doolin Security Savings Bank,
FSB — New Martinsville, WV
First Federal Bank & Trust — Sheridan, WY
Big Horn Federal Savings
Bank — Greybull, WY

The number of mutual savings banks declined significantly in the 1980s, when many failed, merged, or converted to stock-issuing banks. This was in response to rising interest rates that occurred in the late Carter presidency years and asset restrictions put on these savings banks during that time. In the early 1980s, laws restricting what banks could invest in and what interest rates they could pay depositors governed mutual savings banks. Many depositors still preferred to keep their money in a bank that was owned by members who were locally focused and very conservative.

It is best to find a mutual bank that has not changed its bylaws to make a conversion more difficult. Hedge funds and professional investors have been known to spread their money across a number of mutual funds ripe for conversion.

Banks in response can refuse deposits from out-of-town investors. This is done to preserve the profit potential for their local customers. The average person would think any bank would be willing to accept his or her money to become a depositor at their bank. This is not the case with many mutually owned banks.

The ground floor, or initial IPO, is not the only way to profit from mutual-bank investing. As stated earlier, some mutual banks convert in steps. They sell a minority stake to the public and later perform a second-step offering. So, any individual can buy shares of a mutual bank that is trading on an exchange before the second-stage offering occurs. Most of the gain from investing in a mutual-bank conversion comes over the long term. The many company-stock repurchase plans and potential takeover possibilities is where most of the long-term gains occur. Any investor can make money on these companies by simply buying shares after the bank becomes publically traded. But why not also try to get the initial pop in these conversions by having an account at the bank and participating in the IPO?

If you live in an area where there is a mutually owned savings bank, try to open an account at the bank. I recommend opening a Certificate of Deposit account at the bank. CD accounts typically renew automatically at the bank. A passbook or savings account may require an annual deposit to keep from becoming inactive. All mutual banks will have dormancy requirements. (An account becomes dormant if there is no activity in it over a period of time.) CD accounts, which typically renew by themselves, don't require any annual activity.

It is imperative to keep accounts active, because the bank is required by state law to send deposits to the unclaimed property division of the state if they do not hear from the owner over a two- or three-year period. Therefore, if your account is not updated, you may lose your account at the bank and lose the right to buy stock in the bank if it ever decides to convert and go public.

Some banks will accept opening accounts by mail. This has been tougher to accomplish since the establishment of the Patriot Act in 2001 after the 9/11 attacks. This act was created to prevent terrorism and ensure proper identification of individuals trying to open bank accounts.

An interested investor should call these mutual banks and ask to open an account with them. They may require an investor to come to the bank in person with proper identification. I have received many letters stating this fact. If that is the case, plan a trip or vacation in the respective area and open an account. You will be glad you did if the bank ever converts and goes public.

One other tip is to open an account in these banks with a deposit of at least $5,000. In the 1990s, many depositors were able to receive full share allocations of the bank's IPO with a deposit of only fifty dollars in their account. But today there are too many investors trying to buy stock in these IPO conversions. To ensure you get a significant allocation in the offering, I recommend making a larger initial deposit at the bank if possible.

The size of your deposit will determine how many shares you get in the IPO if bank members oversubscribe the stock offering. Depositors at the bank also have priority in getting stock in the IPO over borrowers at the bank. You must have some money at the bank to participate in the conversion.

My advice is to try to open as many accounts as your financial situation allows. It is a numbers game, and the more accounts you have, the better your chance of participating in a possible mutual conversion. But even if you cannot participate in the conversion, still consider buying shares in these mutual bank stocks after they convert. You will be glad you did.

CHAPTER 7

ON THE ROAD AGAIN: HOW I OPENED SOME OF MY BANK ACCOUNTS

When I started opening bank accounts after the Fort Wayne Home Loan stock offering in 1993, it was fairly easy to become a depositor at most mutual savings banks. Since there was no Google, I did most of my research at the local library. *SNL Financial* was also a great source of information in providing information on mutual stock conversions. They printed a monthly hard copy publication with detailed information on the industry. Today, they provide much of this information online. I paid *SNL Financial* for the master list of all mutually owned savings banks. As I stated earlier, most of these banks were located in the northeastern region. However, a fair amount of these banks are also located in Midwestern states. Today, there are 577 mutual banks located in forty-four states. The states with the most mutual banks are Massachusetts (111), Illinois (50) Ohio (47), and Pennsylvania (46). As of 2011, mutual banks had total assets of $209 billion. The median mutual bank had assets of $191 million.

Some of these mutual banks have assets as small as $30 million, while others have over $2 billion in assets. I have had the best success investing in banks with assets over $500 million. That being said, I would still open an account in any mutual savings banks that have at least $100 million in assets. I would pass on opening accounts at banks under $100 million due to limited prospects of a bank with such few assets being acquired by a larger institution down the road. Remember that the long-term appeal of this investment is that a larger institution may acquire the bank three to five years down the road. I also try to make sure the bank is not losing money and find out what discount-to-book value the bank shares are being offered to depositors.

Once I had the master list of banks that were still mutually owned, I ventured out to open as many banks as I could. I started in Indiana and drove forty miles north to Angola, Indiana to open an account at First Federal Savings Bank. I then proceeded to drive to Hammond, Munster, Richmond, Logansport, and then south to Terre Haute and Martinsville. I tried to open a CD account in any bank on the list that I could. I encourage you to do the same in your respective hometown areas.

Of course if you already live in the Boston or Chicago area, it is much easier for you to participate in this investment thesis than someone from California or Arizona. This investment thesis is a numbers game, meaning the more bank accounts that you can open the better your chances will be to participate in a potential IPO conversion.

I have many funny stories and memories of opening up various bank accounts through the years. In the late 90s, a client and I drove to western Indiana and the Chicago area in an attempt to open bank accounts. In the '90s, there was a sign by the teller or desk that said all accounts are verified by CHEX Systems. The bank would verify your Social Security number for fraud purpose. This nice older lady came back and said, "Are you guys drug dealers? We are showing you have opened six accounts at different banks in the past two days. What is going on here?" She eventually opened the account after we explained that we were just opening the account for potential conversion opportunities.

You never know which bank will convert and go public. Some banks will never convert. The goal is to open as many accounts as you possibly can. It only takes one big win for you to become hooked on this investment thesis.

CHAPTER 8

HOW DOES AN IPO WORK?

W hen an investor tries to invest in a typical IPO, he or she contacts his or her broker or adviser and hopes that the broker's firm is able to get him or her shares of the offering. Firms like Goldman Sachs and JPMorgan are typically the lead underwriters of the offering. Smaller firms like Stifel and Raymond James may be in the selling group and provide shares to their clientele. The problem with most IPOs is that the small investor will have difficulty getting a meaningful number of shares if the stock is poised to do well in the aftermarket.

The underwriters will try to find a price that the owners or prior investors are happy to receive. But they also need to bring the offering at a price where the new investors feel they are making a good investment. Most of these firms give their institutional or larger investors a greater allocation than the retail or individual investor. Mutual and hedge funds also get preferential treatment in the allocation process over the average investor. This is due to these companies having bigger accounts at these firms. They will take shares of every offering the firm may have. Some will be good and others bad. But these accounts will participate in every deal these firms are in. Most investors will not want to participate in every deal that becomes available. This is one of the reasons that individuals get very few shares in the IPO allocation process. This lack of share allocation is why the average investor cannot make a significant return on most new stock IPOs.

That is why a bank mutual stock conversion or IPO is such an attractive investment opportunity for the average investor. In these offerings, an investor can purchase as little as one hundred shares or $1000, up to in some cases sixty thousand shares or $600,000. However, an investor would never be able to participate in a traditional syndicate led hot IPO (Snap Chat is a good example) and expect to receive an allocation of even in the amount of $50,000.

In a bank mutual IPO, there is one underwriting firm whose basic function is to oversee the allocation of their shares mainly to the depositors of the bank. Remember that the depositors are the owners of these savings banks. The underwriters of these bank offerings will send you an order form to complete and return to them with an indication of the dollar amount you are willing to invest. They will also include a prospectus explaining the risks and terms of the offering. Do not be overly worried about the risks stated in the prospectus. Attorneys will state any and all possible risks in the prospectus. I always look at two sections inside these prospectuses. The first section is how many shares the insiders at the bank are purchasing in the stock offering. Insiders are the bank president and directors. You want to see that these individuals are purchasing a significant number of shares in the stock offering. Local bank officers do not typically make a huge salary. If the insiders are investing a significant portion of their net worth in the conversion offering that is a positive sign they believe this is an attractive investment.

The second section is what the book value of the bank will be at various offering levels. There will be a minimum and maximum offering range of shares to be offered. The bank needs to reach the minimum offering level for the IPO to commence. The maximum level is the largest amount of shares the bank is offering to depositors. The higher the range of shares issued, the larger the book value for the bank. Book value of a company is the net asset value of the bank. This is typically also the difference between a company's assets minus liabilities.

The beauty of the mutual conversions is that after the offering takes place, the bank is flush with all of this cash from the new investors. These offerings are typically priced at about 60 percent of the bank's book value. So, you as a new investor are buying a bank at a 40 percent discount to its peers and own an asset that has a lot of cash on their balance sheet. Not a bad scenario for future investors.

Once you receive this order form, you typically have three to four weeks to return it to the bank with your indication of shares. You will write a personal check payable directly to the bank, not the brokerage firm or underwriter. If you want to purchase these shares from an IRA account, you must immediately forward this signed and completed order form to your brokerage firm, which acts as the custodian to your IRA. The brokerage firms will then take money from your IRA and forward it to the bank on your behalf.

To complete the order form, you will need your Social Security number, the account number of your CD or savings account at the mutual bank, and how you want your shares titled. You will also send a check back to the bank for the full amount you wish to purchase. If the shares are oversubscribed, you may not get all of the shares you want in the offering. This is where your account size at the bank will help you acquire a greater allocation of shares in the offering. There will be a closing date on the order form. You must return your order form by that date. I also recommend overnight delivery of your order form and check. This ensures tracking, and you will know that the bank has received your order.

After the closing date, it will take the underwriting firm about three weeks to close the offering and determine allocation of shares to the depositors. The underwriting firm will have a stock center phone number for you to call and ask for your share allocations. The stock offering will commence trading on the stock market a few days after you receive your share allocations. The stock will then begin trading typically on the NASDAQ exchange. The NASDAQ exchange gives many firms the opportunity to make a market in the stock for their clients. Making a market will help provide liquidity for a firm's shareholders to buy and sell the stock. Many of these bank offerings will have fairly illiquid (investments with limited or no secondary market) markets. After the first couple days of trading on the exchange, the volume of shares that will trade on the bank stock will be very small. This illiquidity is usually a long-term positive as so few shareholders will sell their stock. With no sellers, the stock price can bid up to higher prices until someone is willing to sell their shares.

Typically, an investor will be very happy when the shares begin to trade. Most bank conversions see an initial appreciation ranging from 15 to 30 percent when the shares begin trading in the public market. I have participated in only one offering where the share price has declined from the initial price. This was in a small bank in Madison, Wisconsin, called Home Savings and Loan. I never should have participated in this offering. The bank inserted an extra page of risk stating that the bank had not made money in years and was not projected to make a profit for several years. The bank practically told investors not to participate in the offering due to the excess risk at the bank. I should have passed on participating in the offering. The stock opened at $9.50 and proceeded to drop to $8. However today, less than two years later, the stock trades at over $11 per share. This is above the $10 per share offering price. So, even this troubled bank's share price has rebounded to be a profitable investment.

An investor can sell his or her stock and make the quick initial profit or continue to hold as a long-term investment. Some depositors may sell a portion of their shares if they received a full allocation for diversification purposes. Holding on to these shares is the best option if possible. But if an investor is borrowing money to purchase the maximum shares allowed, it may make sense to sell enough of shares at a gain to pay off the amount he or she owes the bank and keep his or her profit in the stock.

Although there are no guarantees in any stock investment, mutual savings banks that go public have shown tremendous gains in their stock price compared to the initial IPO price. Here are some of the reasons for this outperformance. Mutual savings banks have book value (a company's assets/liabilities) that is mainly cash, and this cash remains property of the bank after the stock offering. Thus, you will always be buying shares for less than the book value of the new publicly traded bank. Mutual savings banks are also typically smaller banks that are located in key markets in various cities and towns. They soon become takeover targets by larger banks that are looking to get in their market area. These buyouts cannot take place until three years after the stock conversion. But if they are bought out, this can be at three to four times higher than the IPO price depositors paid for their shares. Management of the new bank has the ability to set the IPO price below the bank's book value. Management of the new bank after one year can start buying back significant shares of their own stock. This buying pressure also creates an upward movement in the stock price. All of these factors are reasons why there is strong possibility for a depositor to make money in their local bank stock offering.

CHAPTER 9

RISKS VERSUS REWARDS

All investments except short-term CDs, savings accounts, and other insured investments have some degree of risk. Every investor has to understand all the risks associated with any investment decision they make. I see opportunity cost as the biggest risk for individuals who open accounts at these savings banks. No one knows if the bank you open an account in will ever decide to convert and become a public company. Therefore, you could have many thousands of dollars earning a very low interest rate of return. Also, CD rates have been close to 1 percent or less over the last eight years. Many other investments could have generated a return of greater than 1 percent per year. Index or stock mutual funds have a longer-term return higher than 1 percent. The money you deposit in the bank is FDIC insured, so you have no risk of losing your principal by opening CDs or savings accounts at these banks, but an investor would have to wonder if he or she could have achieved a higher return in a different investment class.

Herein lays the biggest risk of this investment thesis. It takes a lot of money to put $5,000 or more in multiple savings banks in an attempt to participate in a potential IPO conversion. As with all investment portfolios, the key to optimum success is proper diversification among all asset classes.

For a portion of an investor's safer or bond investments, I would recommend opening some CDs at any mutual banks that he or she can. Over the past twenty-three years that I have participated in mutual bank conversion IPOs, I have only seen two offerings where the stock price has declined from the $10 offering price. On the other hand, I have participated in many conversions that have done very well in their aftermarket performance. The largest initial gain I have ever been a depositor in was a 55 percent pop on New Alliance Bank of Connecticut on April 2, 2004. An investor was allowed to purchase up to 500,000 dollars' worth of stock in the New Alliance IPO. New Alliance Bank shares were eventually bought out in 2010 by First Niagara Bank shares. This is the big win for the long-term holder of these bank shares—the buyout potential from a larger bank. My personal batting average is over ninety-eight percent in making money in bank conversions. Over the past several years, I have been able to hold many of my mutual savings stocks for the long-term. To defer taxes, I have tried to invest most of my bank conversion inside my IRA. You need to open a self-directed IRA at a brokerage firm that will help you facilitate the purchase if you want to invest in this fashion.

When I began participating in these conversions with our local bank back in 1993, I needed to borrow money to fully participate in the stock conversion. I am not a proponent of using leverage or borrowing money to make investments. Investments financed by debt that do not show a quick appreciation in value can really hurt the borrower. The borrower is required to keep paying interest payments to the bank while waiting for their investment to rise in value. If the investment takes a long time to appreciate or worse never increase in value, the loss is intensified with the debt service. I do, though, encourage depositors at a savings bank to use any possible means to buy the maximum number of shares you can in the conversion offering. I began by borrowing against my house with my first few offerings. Leverage is good only if your investment goes up. In the bank conversions, you will only be borrowing the money for a period of thirty to sixty days. After the conversion, you can sell a portion of your shares to pay off the money that you borrowed to maximize your share purchase. This is the only investment in which I would encourage an investor to use borrowed money to invest. When you use borrowed money, interest is being charged on the money that you borrowed from the bank. In all other investments, there is not an inherent advantage to buying an asset dramatically below what it is worth. So I never advise clients to use leverage for other investment vehicles. Leverage can be a costly lesson if the investment does not appreciate in value. But in my thirty years as an investment adviser, I have never seen an investment with so much upside and limited downside. Where can you make $250,000 or more on a CD deposit at your local bank?

The number of mutual banks that have converted of late has declined dramatically. A decade ago mutual banks converted into public ownership at a rate of seventeen per year. In 2016, only seven mutual conversions took place. Some of these small-town banks also like the autonomy of being independent and may never convert. Many mutual banks do not want to adhere to concerns of future potential shareholders and will remain as a mutual institution as they have for the past one hundred or so years. But there will always be a few of the remaining five hundred or so that may decide to convert.

Finally, there is an opportunity with the Trump administration that some of the challenges of the Dodd-Frank Act may be tweaked for the smaller mutual saving banks. This act was the most sweeping legislation to hit the banking industry since the New Deal. The architects of Dodd-Frank did not allow any input from bank regulators with a familiarity of mutual bank's corporate governance. The act's heightened capital requirements without taking into the account the limitations on mutual banks for raising capital significantly reduced the risk profile of these banks. The cost of compliance has become burdensome to many banks. A possible reduction in regulations on these smaller mutual banks may lead to more possible bank conversions in the future. Other regulations, like the Sarbanes-Oxley Act, were enacted to stop accounting fraud after the Enron and WorldCom scandals. All of these acts had good intentions but have made it much more expensive to become a public company. Many of these regulations are causing leverage buyouts where public companies are reverting back to private ownership. The Trump administration has stated that they will reduce many of these regulations that are restricting small banks and other companies from becoming public companies. If regulations are relaxed, maybe more mutually owned banks will consider going public and give thrift depositors more investment opportunities.

In summary, there are risks in all investments. But to have a CD or savings account in a mutually owned bank to possibly participate an IPO of the bank seems like an attractive alternative for a portion of an investor's safer monies. Investors should consider buying shares of these banks after they go public even if they were not in the IPO. The company share buybacks that occur after one year along with the overall lack of selling by investors are the main reasons I like this thesis. The icing on the cake is when many of these banks convert; they are bought out at a significant multiple to their book value after the three-year exemption ends.

CHAPTER 10

ALWAYS DIVERSIFY YOUR INVESTMENTS

In my thirty years of advising clients on how to invest their money, the key to any successful investment portfolio has been proper asset diversification based on the client's age and risk tolerances. A good adviser must listen to the needs and objectives of his or her clients. Many clients do not have the risk tolerance for aggressive investments. Investors must realize the risks and returns of any investment vehicle they choose and the liquidity of the investment they are making. There are many clients or referrals that come in that I immediately recognize do not have the capacity to experience any decline in their investments. There are no free lunches in life. To get an above-average return, an investor must be able to accept the risks that are associated with his or her investments. By diversifying across asset classes, this risk can be reduced. The number one rule an adviser must master is rule 305: "Know your customer." This rule requires the adviser understand the client's risk tolerance and investment objectives.

For example, many advisers sell illiquid investments such as annuities and private placements to their clients. Annuities (which are contracts with a life-insurance company) can be very expensive illiquid investments. Annuities are touted on many TV commercials as a cure-all for retired investors. Why then are these annuity contracts that one must sign at purchase as thick as a Bible? The average adviser may not even fully understand all the nuances of the annuity. The biggest negative of an annuity is that an investor cannot get out of most these contracts without paying a significant surrender charge. When an investor buys an annuity, he or she may be forced into staying in the contract for as long as ten to fifteen years or pay significant penalties to get out of the investment. Being tied up into an investment with no access to your money is never a good investment. The only annuities I have used through the years were fixed annuities where an investor received a stated return for the term of the contract. In 2008, many insurance companies offered ten-year fixed rates at almost 7 percent. That is an attractive investment that makes sense for a portion of an individual's safer investment allocation, but every investor must understand the negatives of each investment. Annuities are not only illiquid; they are the only asset class that does not provide a stepped-up basis when one dies. Thus, your kids will have to pay taxes on the gains from an annuity upon your death, whereas there would be no taxes due on an investment with stepped-up basis. A stepped-up basis is where your heirs inherit an asset at the price or cost basis of your death, not at the price you paid for it. Stocks, bonds and most liquid financial assets have this increase in cost basis upon death; however, annuities do not.

In most cases, the younger the investor, the greater amount of risk he or she can take with his or her investments. My CFP training teaches us to subtract the investor's age from one hundred as a starting point for developing a portfolio mix between safe and growth assets. So, a seventy-year-old investor may only have 30 percent of their portfolio in stocks or growth assets while a thirty-year-old may possibly own 70 or more percent of similar investments. Older investors do not have time on their side to be invested in aggressive stocks if risk assets fall in value later in their lives. Imagine having your entire portfolio in growth investments in 2008. Your entire portfolio could have declined 40 percent. Thus, they must have a more conservative allocation than a younger investor. That being said, everyone needs some growth in his or her portfolio.

For the past thirty years, we have been in a declining interest rate environment. So, any bond has been a successful investment. Interest rates in 1980 were as high as 12 percent on a longer-term bond and 16 percent on a short-term CD. If only an investor back then had been smart enough to buy a thirty-year treasury bond when these rates were that high! With a new presidential administration, we may start to see interest rates increase. Investors must realize that in a rising-interest environment, the value of their longer-term bonds can decline if sold prior to maturity. I, therefore, have been a proponent of laddering bond maturities. Using a mix of quality corporate or municipal bonds and preferred stocks has been a good asset mix for an individual's safer investments in his or her portfolio. Municipal bonds have always been the safe asset of choice for millionaires or individuals with significant earned income. But as each of you diversify your bond portfolio; do not forget to add a few mutual bank savings accounts also!

I could write another entire book on all the different investment opportunities. There are private placements, hedge funds, options, commodities, and many other investment vehicles that an investor can purchase. But my point here is to always diversify your investments. Diversification is a risk-management technique that mixes a wide variety of investments within a portfolio. The rationale behind this technique contends that a portfolio constructed of different kinds of investments will, on average, yield higher returns and pose a lower risk than any individual investment found within the portfolio.

Do not put all your eggs in one basket, even bank mutual deposits! One never knows which asset class will be the best performer from year to year. It could be bonds one year; large caps the next, followed by small caps, utilities, or gold and silver. Diversification across all classes is paramount for a successful portfolio. A dollar-cost average or systematic investment approach works especially well for smaller investors. This takes the worry out of thinking that the market may be at a top or ready for a decline. Most people invest in their 401ks through this systematic fashion, but very few do with their other investments. This approach allows investors to take advantage of the peaks and valleys of the financial markets. Surprisingly, timing is the factor that drives portfolio performance. Many investors do not realize this. If you buy stocks during a market downturn, the timing factor works in your favor. So, if timing is one of the key factors to investment performance, there is some luck involved this process.

Fear and greed are two of the investor's emotions that must be controlled to become a successful investor. Do not panic in down markets or get greedy in up markets. However, you want to buy stocks that are going up and have been proven winners versus the lagging companies with low share prices. Early in my career, I sometimes looked for stocks that were depressed in price. The old analogy of "buy low and sell high" does not work for stocks that are declining for a valid reason. These stocks are depressed for a reason. Investors could have thought RadioShack, Enron, and WorldCom were cheap and attractive stocks to buy because their stock price was low. However, all of these companies filed bankruptcy and were eventually worthless. In this case, the investors lost everything. Buying low makes sense if there is an overall market correction, but you do not want to buy a stock just because the share price is low or depressed. The share price is low for a reason. You want to buy the winners or best of breed companies when looking for stocks to invest in.

If an investor had held Amazon, Google, or Visa, they would have been richly rewarded. These companies have continued to expand and grow their business and thus their share prices have increased dramatically. An investor was better off to never sell any of these stocks. That being said, an investor can never go broke taking a profit. One school of thought is to sell half of your position as the stock doubles in value. Then you are playing on the house's money. Selling is a much more difficult decision than buying a stock. When buying a stock, look for companies that have hot products that people are buying. If the company's sales and earnings are growing, usually the stock price will follow in an upward fashion. Imagine the amount of money you could have made in Apple stock when the iPhone was created or when Netflix started their DVD rentals and streaming packages. Buy the leading company in each sector of the marketplace. This means owning the leader of many different categories, such as technology, energy, industrials, financials, and pharmaceutical companies. Look at the longer-term charts of the stocks you are considering buying. You want to see a ten-year upward rising chart to the right. Go to Yahoo Finance and research all these leading companies and see these right upward charts. Some investors rely exclusively on this technical analysis to pick their stocks.

Other financial tips are to become debt free as quickly as possible. One can accomplish this by increasing your income, lowering your expenses, or renegotiating terms with creditors. My first financial goal in life was to pay off my house as soon as possible. It took me three years of constantly making extra principal payments on my mortgage. Try to avoid car loans unless at zero interest. If you have no debt, you will not be forced to make a rash investment decision. You can let your investments grow over the long-term. Also take some risks with your investments. You will never get rich by solely investing in CDs or riskless investments. That does not mean buying speculative or penny stocks. Buy quality investments and lock them away for the long-term. Finally, have fun with your investments. Many people stress out over their investments. If your investments are diversified properly, it can be an enjoyable process to watch your money grow.

In summary, try to get out of debt as soon as possible. Your home mortgage is the only debt you want to have. Maximize your 401k contributions. Be sure to contribute the amount your employer will match. Utilize a Roth 401k or an individual Roth IRA if you qualify. Open 529 accounts to fund your children and grandchildren's college tuition. High net worth individuals can utilize CRT and CLT plans to get money out of their names to avoid estate tax issues. Diversify your investment portfolio based on your age and risk tolerance. Take some risks and have fun with your investments.

CHAPTER 11

FEES

Many TV commercials and investment publications comment on what fees an investor should pay when using a financial adviser and how they may affect long term performance. Passive index funds have been discussed as the most efficient way to invest in 2017. Granted, the fees on these investments have dropped to practically nothing, at less than 0.15 of 1 percent. If an investor is starting out or investing in his or her retirement plan, there is nothing wrong with using an index fund or ETF through Vanguard or other companies. However, the investor must have the patience to ride out market declines and not chase hot or risky investments. Greed and fear are the characteristics every investor must be able to deal with. For busy professionals or individuals who do not have the time to follow and develop their own investment portfolio, it makes sense to use a financial adviser.

When choosing a financial adviser, look for someone who has had success and with whom you feel comfortable. Interview various advisers and see what each has to offer. Make sure your adviser is affiliated with a firm with on line access to monitor their investments and is a member of the SIPC, the Securities Investor Protection Corporation. The SIPC protection protects the cash and securities in your account if the brokerage firm fails. Madoff investors wished they looked for this designation before they invested with his firm.

One other piece of advice when searching for a financial adviser is to ask him or her to show you some of his or her own personal investments or returns. Many advisers lose a lot of their own money with aggressive trading and bad investments. Verifying that an adviser is successful with his or her own investments is a good indication that he or she will advise you properly with your portfolio. Look for an adviser with a CFP credential or at least one who has several years of experience. Run a background check on your adviser on FINRA.org. Beware of market-beating embellishment, and check to ensure the credentials the person claims to have are current.

When you pick an adviser, find out how he or she is compensated. In the 1980s when I started as an adviser, almost everyone charged clients commissions for their various transactions. Today the big craze is fee only, where a client pays no commissions but an annual fee on the assets they have with an adviser. Many investors think the fee-only route is the cheapest and best way for them to invest. If I had every client in a fee-only relationship, my income would more than double what I earn today. If an investor is just looking to buy CDs, municipal bonds, or preferred or interest-bearing investments, he or she is much better off buying these in a traditional commission-based account. Weekly CDs and short-term corporate bonds are available with no inherent commission the client will pay. Many firms also underwrite new issue preferred stocks that come available at $25 per share. The client at $25 per share with no commission can buy these. The company issuing the bond or new issue preferred pays the adviser. I have many retired clients who are solely looking for income and buy these types of investments. These clients pay practically no fees when buying these types of investments. Many independent advisers do not have access to the syndicate preferred offerings and cannot provide these investments to their clients. I encourage all investors to look for these types of investments as a way to reduce their fees.

With the proposed DOL Fiduciary Rule that was to take place early in 2017, all IRA and retirement plan investors were going to be forced into some type of fee or advisory relationship. It frustrated many of my preferred or income buyers that they would have to pay me a 1 percent fee on their IRA accounts when they were actually not paying any out-of-pocket fees to invest. One couple in particular came in when they realized that they each may have to pay me $10,000 in annual fees for their IRA account when they have paid me nothing in commission or fees when buying their new issue preferreds over the last eight years. The implementation of the DOL Fiduciary Rule has been delayed as of this date. We, therefore, do not know the ramifications of this proposal on the advisory business. So, at times, fee only can be a much more expensive advisory relationship. If an investor is buying stocks or growth assets, it may make more sense to be in a fee-only or fee-based relationship. Actively traded accounts almost always should be in a fee-based relationship to avoid excessive commissions on trades. On the other hand, if an individual is going to buy Amazon, Google, or another big-name stock that he or she plans to hold for many years, he or she would be better off paying a one-time commission versus an annual fee to hold a stock he or she does not plan on selling.

It is paramount to discuss all these situations when you are interviewing advisers. Fee only may not be cheapest way to invest with an adviser. Today, a local adviser was on his weekly TV show discussing the benefits of owning annuities. If any of his clients knew how much commission he made when selling them the annuity, I doubt they would be too happy. Outside of fixed annuities when interest rates are higher, I cannot see a reason to own an annuity. The fees inside the contract are just too high. Annuities' illiquid nature, lack of step-up basis, and high surrender charges do not make them the asset of choice for most investors. Motivational speaker, Tony Robbins and Vanguard mutual fund founder, Jack Bogel were quoted in a recent Money Magazine article on 4/14/2017 that fees mean everything when evaluating performance with your investments over the long term. My only thought on that topic is for investors to truly understand the fees they are paying their advisers and see if fee only or commission products are cheaper for them. As I said earlier, if an individual feels comfortable investing on his or her own, he or she can do so using passive index funds. But buying and holding Amazon over the last ten years has dramatically outperformed an index fund. When the markets get tough and the investor wants to bail at the worst time, that is when a relationship with a financial adviser can make sense. Just make sure the adviser's fee or commission relationship is the best one for you.

CHAPTER 12

2016: The Year of Change

The calendar year 2016 will be remembered as the year of change. It could also be referred as the year of the underdog. It started with the Brexit vote in Europe. This was the June 23, 2016, referendum whereby British citizens voted to exit the European Union. Odds the day before were 6 to 1 against a vote for change by the Britain population. It continued into this fall with the United States presidential election.

Hillary Clinton had a 75 percent probability of winning the day before the election. Many pundits believed Trump's volatile nature would turn off voters. How could these experts and polls have such bad information?

The change movement also carried over into sports. The Chicago Cubs won a World Series title in baseball after a drought of more than one hundred years. Our local college basketball team, the Fort Wayne Mastodons, beat Indiana University from the Big Ten in a college basketball game. Will this change environment continue over into the investment industry?

There are pundits who make predictions in all areas of life. Most predictions are usually wrong, so do not change your investment strategy because someone preaches doom and gloom. Many doomsayers have been calling for a financial collapse for decades. It seldom happens, but somehow these individuals still continue to have a bully pulpit in the press even though their calls are almost always wrong. Boy, do I miss people like the late Mark Haines from CNBC who would call a spade a spade.

Since the future is impossible to predict, investors really need to revisit the chapter on diversification of your investments. Everyone wants an investment to have practically no risk and high returns. Unfortunately, there are no free lunches where an investor receives a great return with little or no risk. But the investment thesis of mutual bank investing has practically no downside and the potential for substantial gains down the road.

All investors have had some low-risk investments. Most people have a checking or savings account at a bank where they park money to pay bills. Why not then keep some of these monies in your local mutual savings bank? This deposit may give you the possibility of someday participating in the bank's IPO. There is no other investment vehicle that allows an investor to leverage a $5,000 deposit at your local bank into the possibility of purchasing up to $600,000 worth of a hot IPO. By participating in a mutual savings bank conversion, you will be buying an asset below book value that has just had a major influx of cash from the stock offering. Sounds like a pretty good long-term investment.

After one year, your bank will probably begin stock buybacks to further push up the share price. The bank has all this extra cash and has to invest it somewhere. Why not put it in a bank that is trading below book value? These are reasons there are so few sellers in these bank conversions. The big kicker takes place after three years of being a public company when a larger bank may come in and acquire your local bank. All of these are positive outcomes for your investment in your mutual savings bank. I encourage you to look in your local area to see if there is a mutual savings bank in which to open an account. I am sure you will be glad you did if the bank ever decides to go public.

In conclusion, I want to summarize a recent IPO offering I had this past year. Harbor One

Bancorp (symbol HONE), a recent Massachusetts mutual bank, converted and went public on June 2, 2016. I had a deposit of $10,000 in the bank. This deposit allowed me to purchase sixty thousand shares or $600,000 worth of newly issued stock. No individual investor is ever given the opportunity to buy $600,000 worth of any other potential hot IPO. Harbor One was a larger savings bank with assets over $2 billion in the bank. Larger banks usually have bigger pops than smaller bank conversions in the aftermarket if they go public. Harbor One began the day trading around $13 per share, a 30 percent pop. But the real beauty of this investment was that as of this writing, on May 4, 2017, Harbor One Bancorp was trading at $21.30 per share. That is a gain of over 100 percent in six months. I know of no other investment thesis that has this type of upside. I will go to the grave stating that this is the best investment opportunity available to the average investor. You can bank on it!

While finishing my book, I had a client call me about buying shares of his restaurant's insurance company, Illinois Casualty Corporation. They received an order with the opportunity to purchase up to $2 million worth of stock. I had never participated in an insurance company conversion. In looking at the prospectus, I saw that the book value of Illinois Casualty (symbol ICCH) was $15 per share versus the $10 per share offering price. This share offering price disparity relative to the insurance company's book value is what usually occurs in the bank conversions.

I advised my clients to participate in the offering. The first trade when ICCH went public was $16 per share. My clients made a 60 percent profit on this investment within a month. If these clients invested $2 million dollars in this offering they would have made over a million dollars in a month!

This transaction reaffirms my view that investors should be participating in any and all mutual conversions. They may be banks, credit unions, or insurance companies. But when given the opportunity, the investor must send money in to participate in these type of stock offerings. In most cases, the investor should purchase the maximum number of shares offered or that he or she can afford.

Finally, on April 21, 2017, the largest one-day pop in a bank conversion occurred that I have ever seen. Unfortunately, I did not have an account in the savings bank in Yorktown Heights in New York. But the stock went from an IPO offer price of $10 and at the end of trading was at $16.50. An investor could have had a one-day gain of 65 percent on a possible investment of $300,000. The investor who received a full share allocation had a one day profit of $195,000. Not a bad day of work for the average investor! The proof is in the pudding that this investment thesis works. Given today's decrease in regulations, the potential gains in mutual conversions may even be at a sweet spot. You can bank on it!

About the Author

Tim Rooney is a Financial Adviser/ CFP® in Fort Wayne, Indiana. He is a Senior Vice President and Branch Manager at Stifel. He joined Stifel in 2001, after working as an adviser at Baird and Shearson/Smith Barney since 1986. He has won local stock picking contests and  has been a perennial member of the Stifel Chairman's Council since 2001. Mr. Rooney manages over 250 million dollars of client assets for more than 750 households. He graduated from Purdue University with honors in Management and Finance. Mr. Rooney is a married father of three children. He is an active community member in Fort Wayne where he serves on various boards and coaches youth basketball.

For more information on mutual bank conversions go to howtobankonit.com. Mr. Rooney can also be reached at rooneyt@stifel.com for more information.

Made in the USA
Middletown, DE
22 April 2018